SISTER ACT & SISTER ACT 2:
BACK IN THE HABIT

T0057508

Disney characters and artwork © Disney Enterprises, Inc.

ISBN 978-1-4803-4311-5

TOUCHSTONE PICTURES MUSIC & SONGS, INC.

DISTRIBUTED BY

HAL•LEONARD®
CORPORATION
7777 W. BLUEMOUND RD. P.O. BOX 13819 MILWAUKEE, WI 53213

Visit Hal Leonard Online at
www.halleonard.com

AIN'T NO MOUNTAIN HIGH ENOUGH

Words and Music by NICKOLAS ASHFORD
and VALERIE SIMPSON

Moderately slow

Now, if you need me, call me. No mat-ter where you
I set you free? I told you you could

are, no mat-ter how far. Don't wor-ry ba-
al - ways count on me. And from that day on,

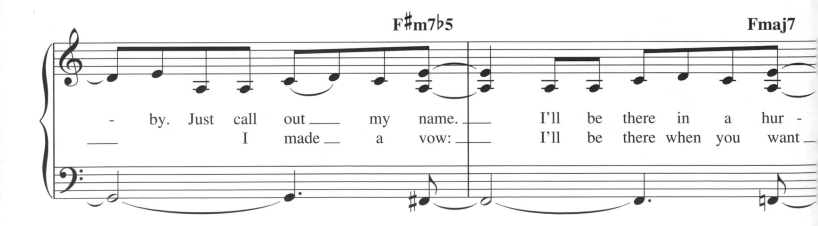

- by. Just call out my name. I'll be there in a hur-
I made a vow: I'll be there when you want

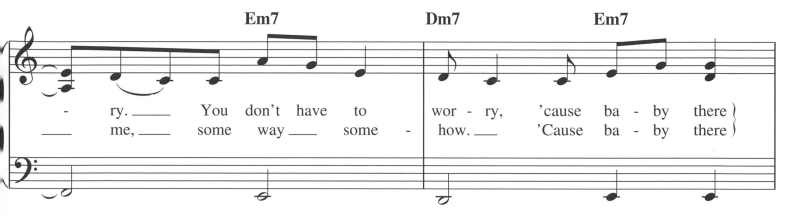

Em7 · Dm7 · Em7

- ry. _____ You don't have to wor - ry, 'cause ba - by there
_____ me, _____ some way _____ some - how. _____ 'Cause ba - by there

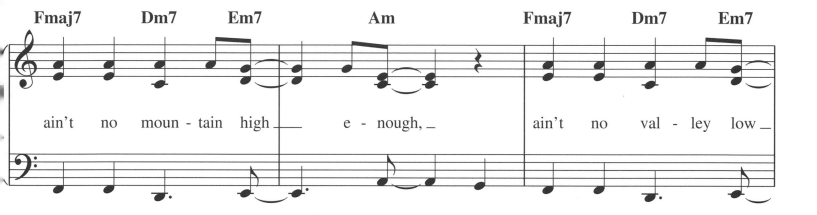

Fmaj7 · Dm7 · Em7 · Am · Fmaj7 · Dm7 · Em7

ain't no moun - tain high _____ e - nough, _ ain't no val - ley low _

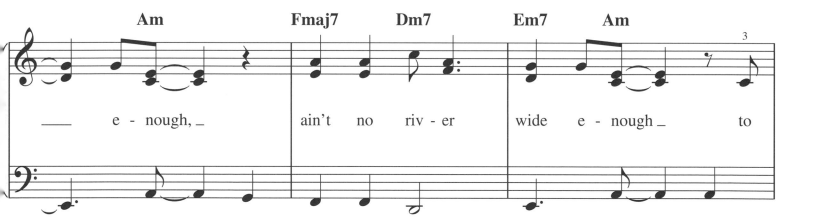

Am · Fmaj7 · Dm7 · Em7 · Am

_____ e - nough, _ ain't no riv - er wide e - nough _ to

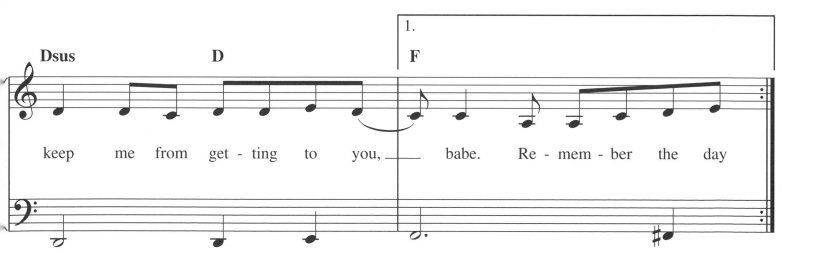

Dsus · D · 1. · F

keep me from get - ting to you, _____ babe. Re - mem - ber the day

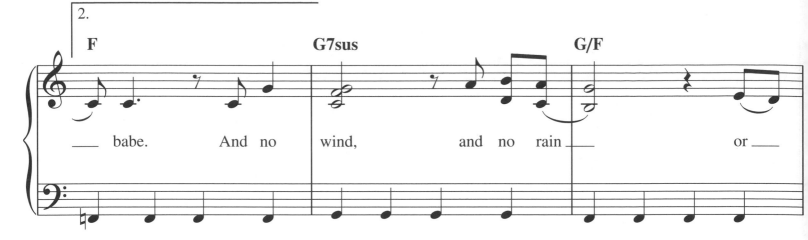

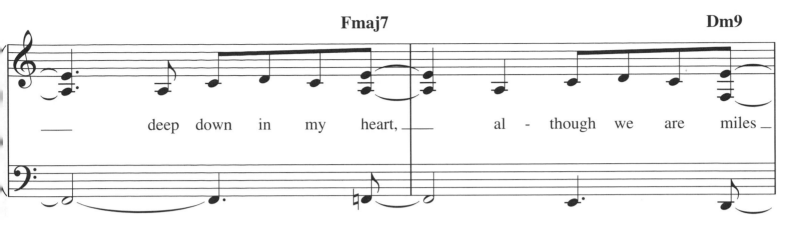

deep down in my heart,___ al - though we are miles___

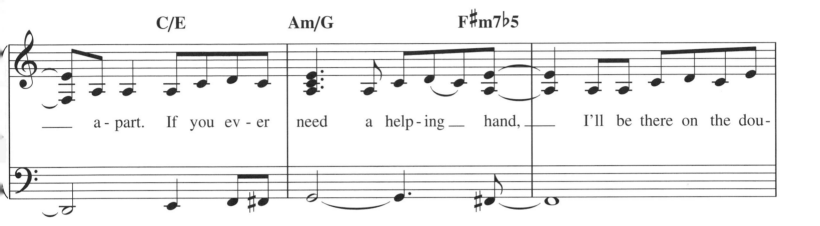

___ a - part. If you ev - er need a help-ing ___ hand, ___ I'll be there on the dou-

ble ___ just as fast as I can. ___ Don't you know that there ain't no moun-tain high ___

___ e - nough, ___ ain't no val - ley low ___ e - nough, ___

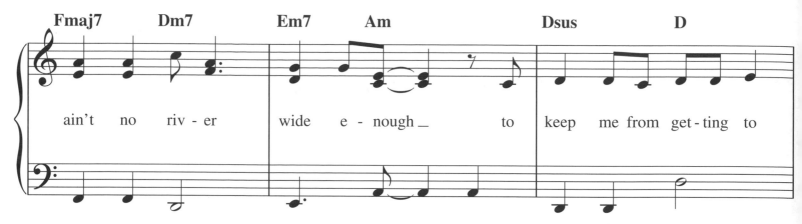

ain't no riv - er wide e - nough ___ to keep me from get - ting to

you, babe. Ain't no moun - tain high e - nough,

ain't no val - ley low e - nough, ain't no riv - er wide e - nough to

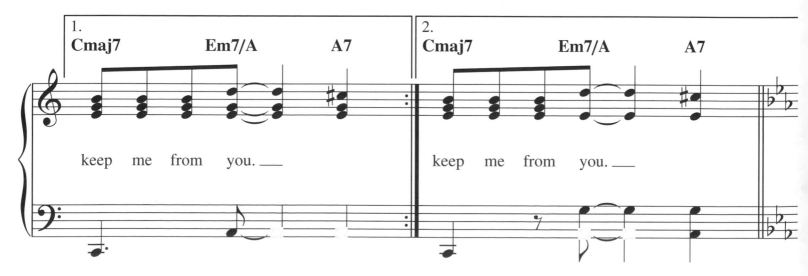

keep me from you. ___ keep me from you. ___

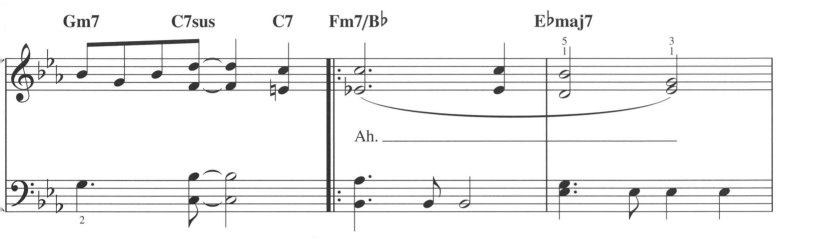

Ah. _____

Noth-ing can keep __ me, keep me from you. __ Ain't no moun - tain

Repeat and Fade

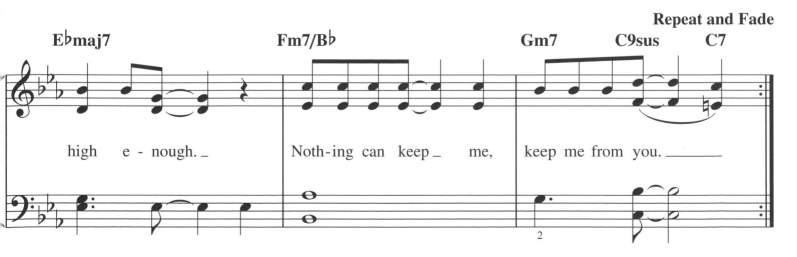

high e - nough. __ Noth-ing can keep __ me, keep me from you. _____

A DEEPER LOVE

Words and Music by ROBERT CLIVILLES
and DAVID COLE

Bright dance tempo

Peo-ple, let ___ me tell you. I work hard ___ ev-er-y day. ___

___ I get up ___ out of bed, I put on my clothes, ___ 'cause

I've got bills ___ to pay. ___ Now, it ain't ___ eas - y, but I don't

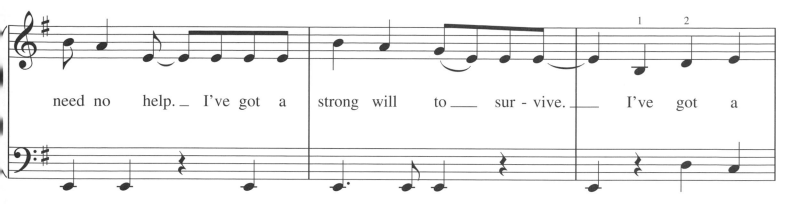

need no help. __ I've got a strong will to __ sur - vive. __ I've got a

G/B

Cmaj7

C/D

deep - er __ love, __ a deep - er __ love, __ a deep - er love __ in -

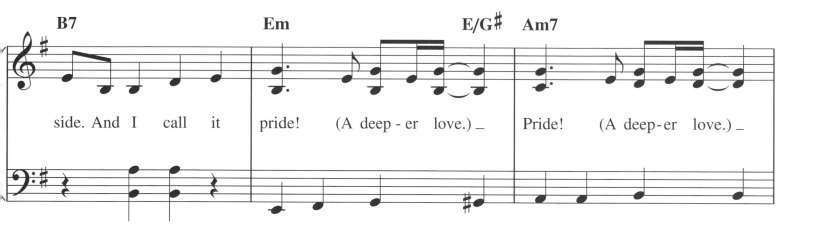

B7

Em

E/G♯ Am7

side. And I call it pride! (A deep - er love.) __ Pride! (A deep - er love.) __

Em

E/G♯ Am7 Bm7

Dm7

G7

Pride! (A deep - er love. __ Whoa, whoa, whoa.) It's the pow - er that gives you the

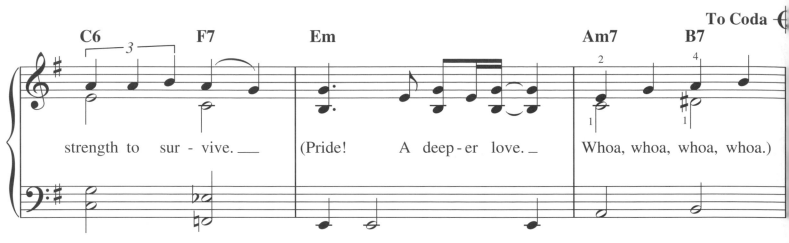

strength to sur - vive. ___ (Pride! A deep-er love. _ Whoa, whoa, whoa, whoa.)

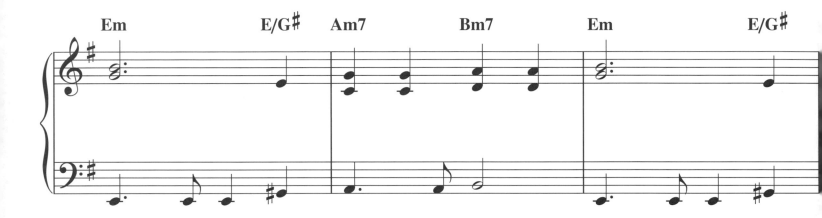

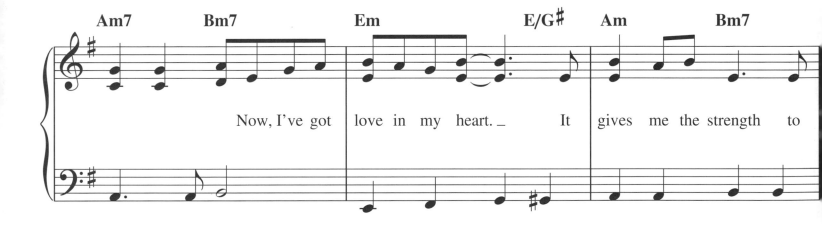

Now, I've got love in my heart. ___ It gives me the strength to

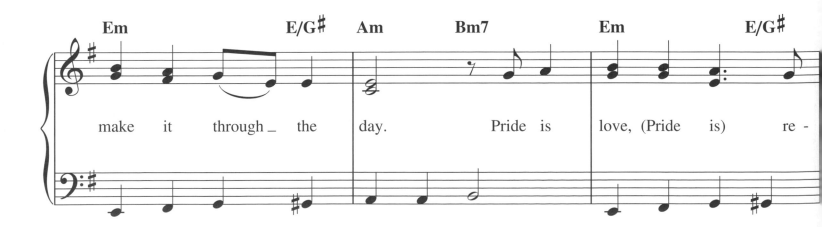

make it through _ the day. Pride is love, (Pride is) re -

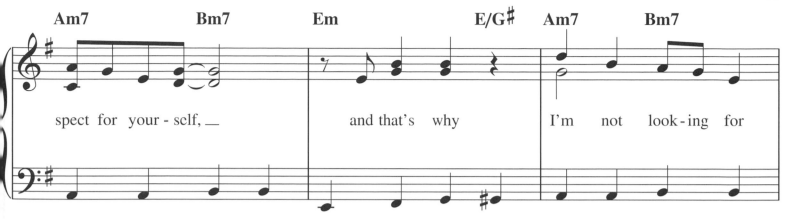

spect for your - self, __ and that's why I'm not look-ing for

hand - outs. Char - i - ty, wel - fare I don't need. Steal - in', deal - in',

not my feel - ing. No back-stab - bin', greed - y, grab - bin',

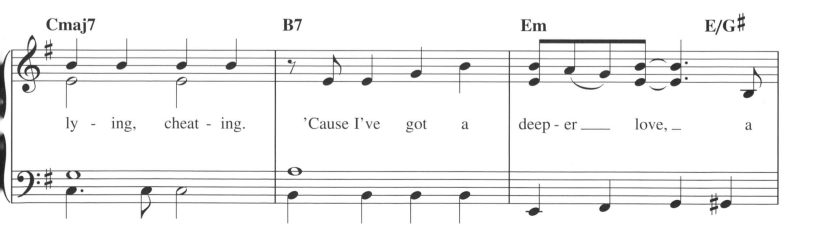

ly - ing, cheat - ing. 'Cause I've got a deep - er __ love, __ a

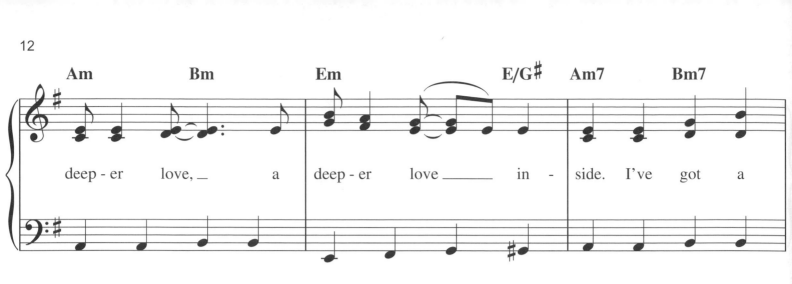

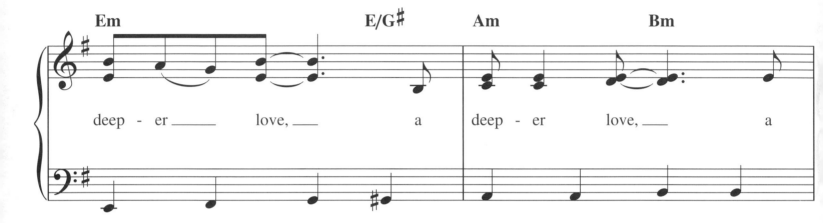

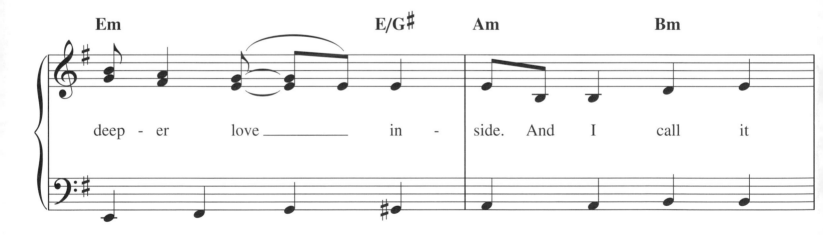

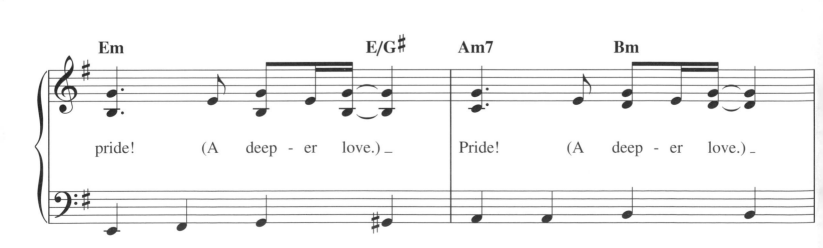

Pride! (A deep-er love. __ Whoa, whoa whoa. It's the

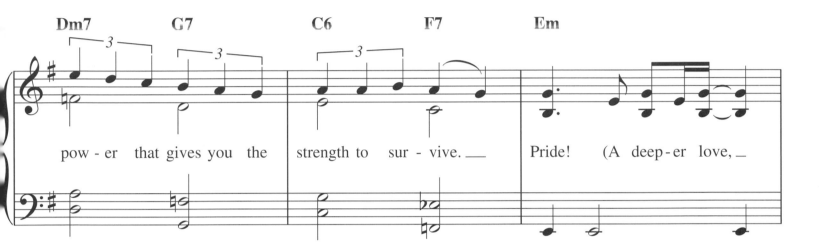

pow-er that gives you the strength to sur-vive. __ Pride! (A deep-er love, __

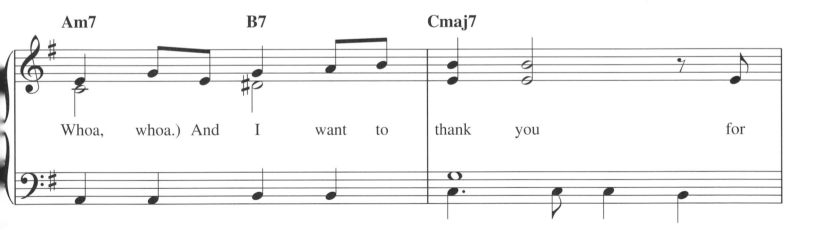

Whoa, whoa.) And I want to thank you for

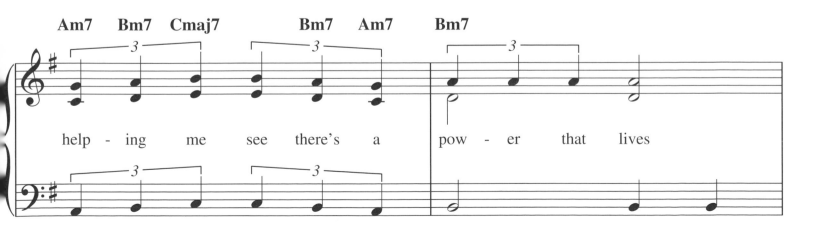

help-ing me see there's a pow-er that lives

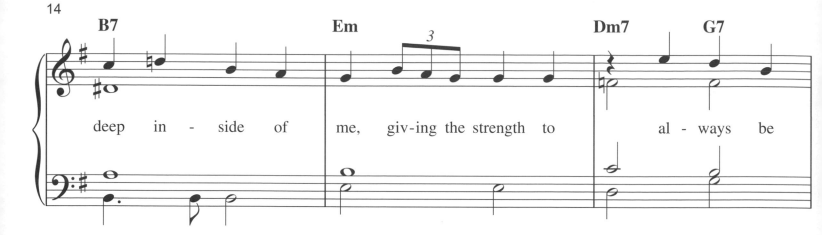

B7   **Em**   **Dm7**   **G7**

deep in - side of me, giv-ing the strength to al - ways be

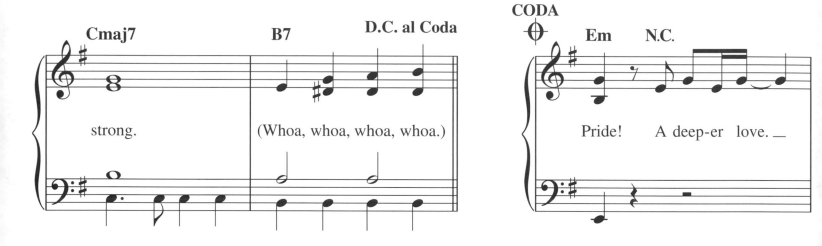

Cmaj7   **B7**   **D.C. al Coda**   **CODA**   **Em**   **N.C.**

strong.   (Whoa, whoa, whoa, whoa.)   Pride! A deep-er love. _

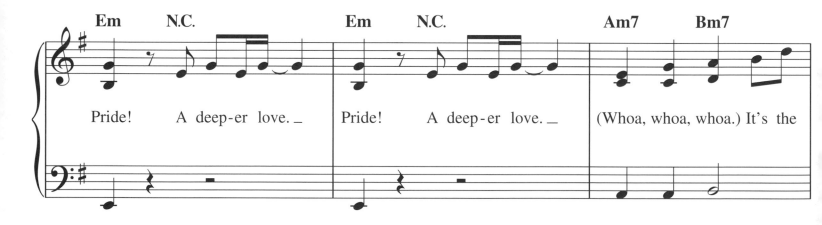

Em   **N.C.**   **Em**   **N.C.**   **Am7**   **Bm7**

Pride! A deep-er love. _   Pride! A deep-er love. _   (Whoa, whoa, whoa.) It's the

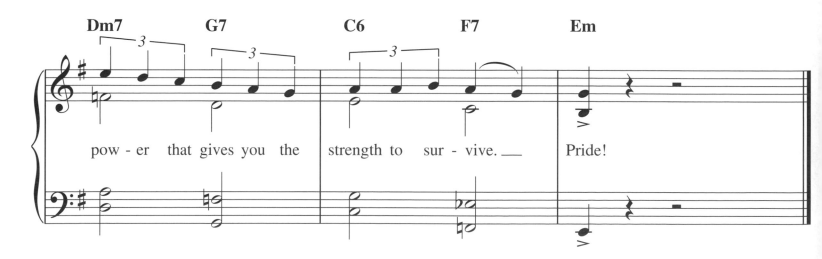

Dm7   **G7**   **C6**   **F7**   **Em**

pow - er that gives you the strength to sur - vive. _ Pride!

HAIL HOLY QUEEN

Words and Music Traditional
Arrangement by MARC SHAIMAN

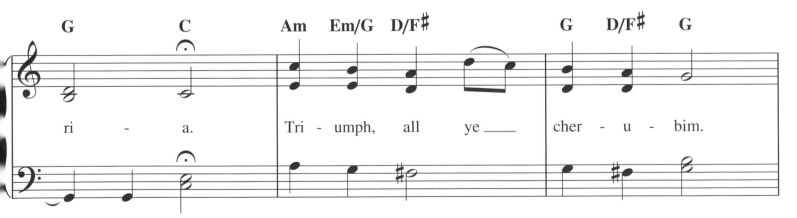

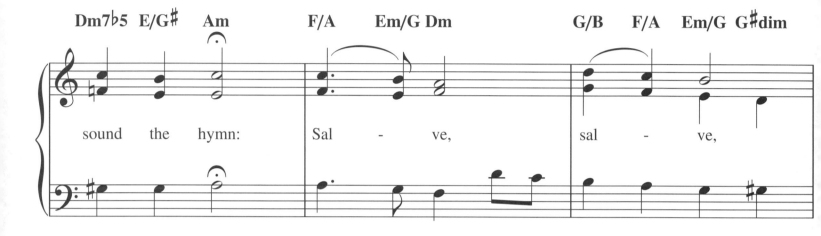

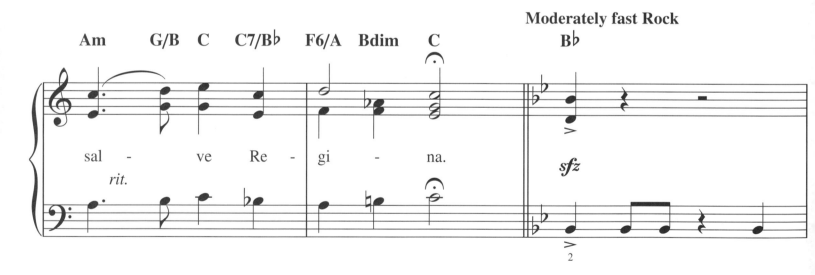

O _____ Ma - ri - a. Hail, _ moth-er of mer - cy ___

and of love, O _____ Ma - ri - a.

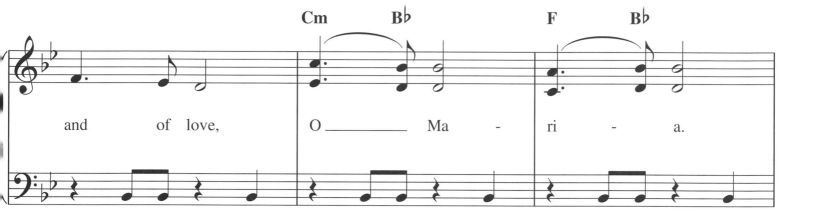

Tri - umph, all ye ___ cher - u - bim. Sing with us, ye ___

ser - a - phim. Heav-en and earth re - sound the hymn:

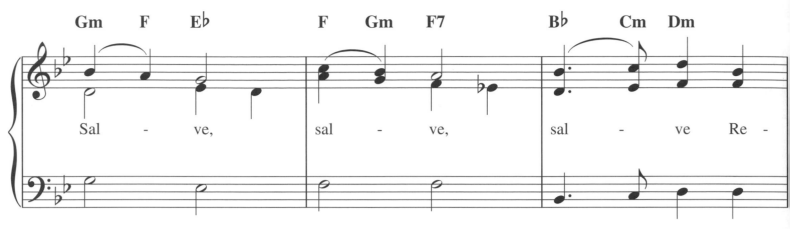

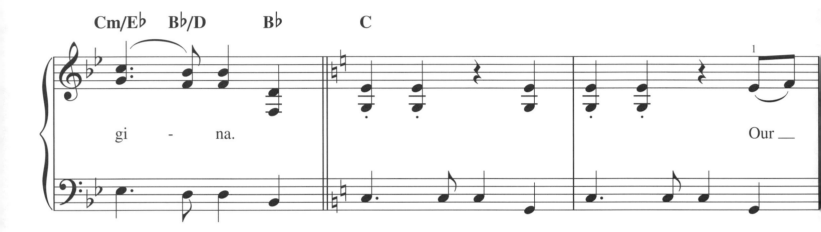

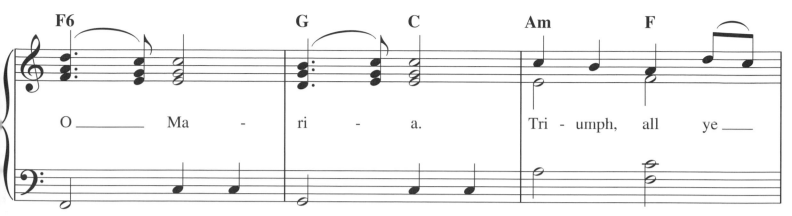

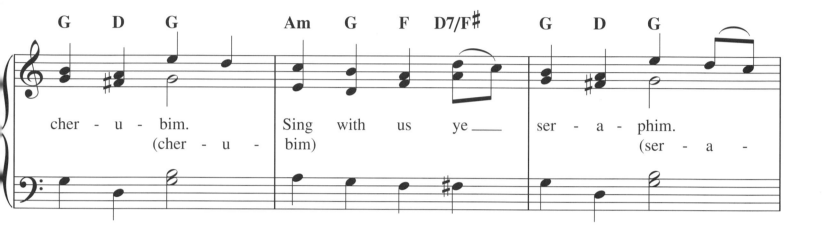

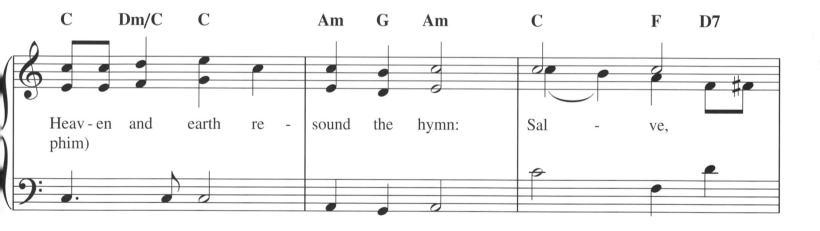

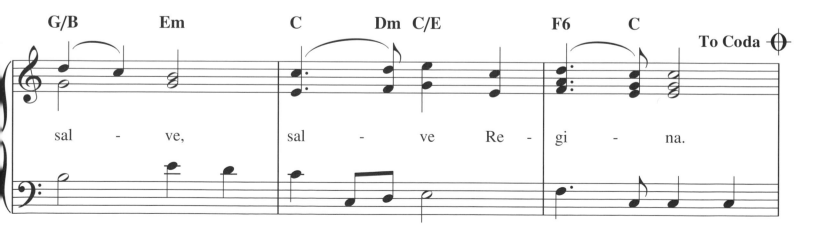

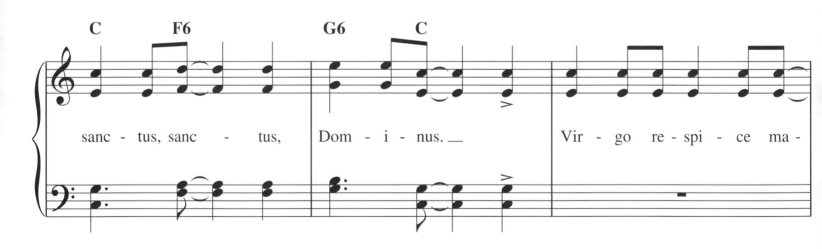

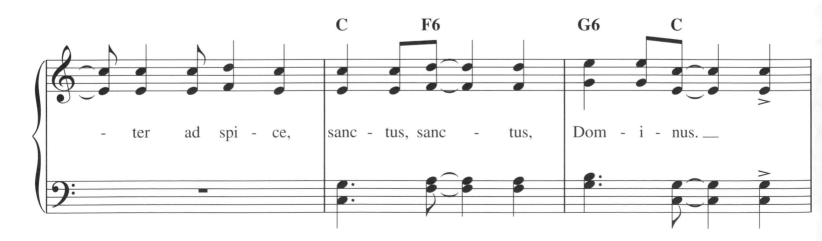

Al - le - lu -

ia. Our ___

D.S. al Coda

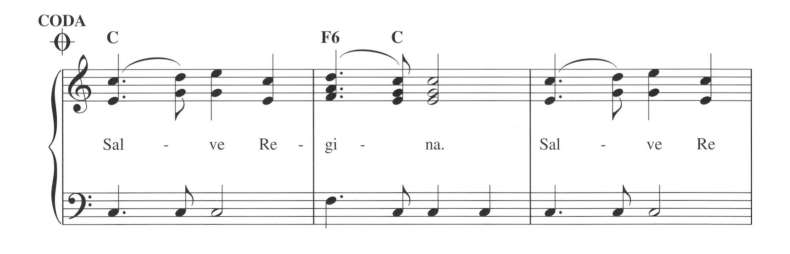

CODA

Sal - ve Re - gi - na. Sal - ve Re -

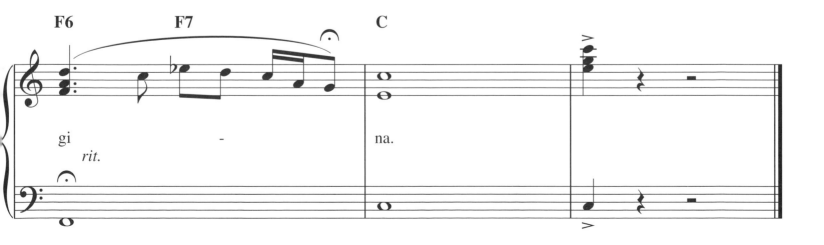

gi - na.

rit.

HIS EYE IS ON THE SPARROW

Words by CIVILLA D. MARTIN
Music by CHARLES H. GABRIEL

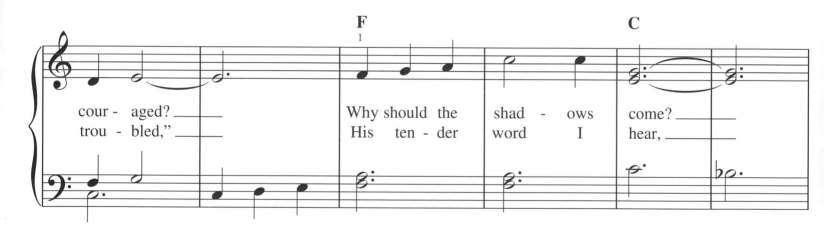

heav'n and home, when Je - sus is ____ my por - tion, ____
doubts and fears. Though by the path ____ He lead - eth, ____

____ my con - stant friend ____ is He. His eye is
____ but one step I ____ may see.

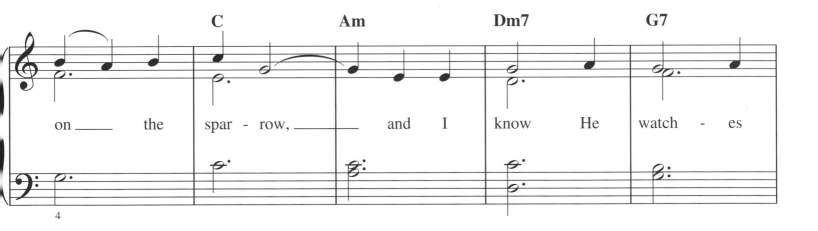

on ____ the spar - row, ____ ____ and I know He watch - es

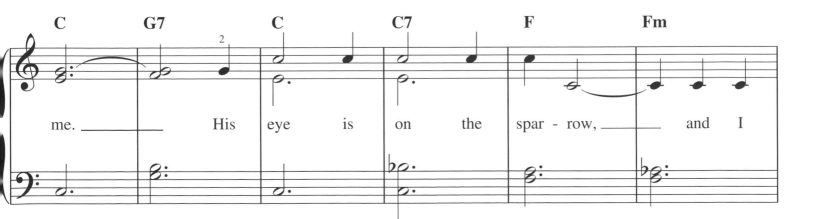

me. ____ ____ His eye is on the spar - row, ____ and I

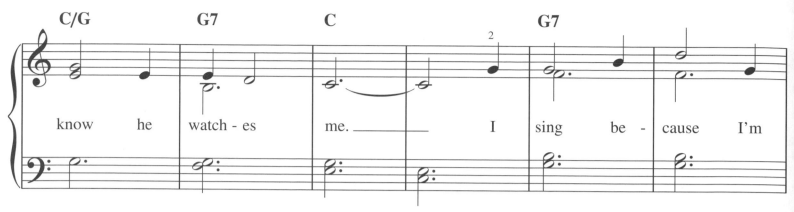

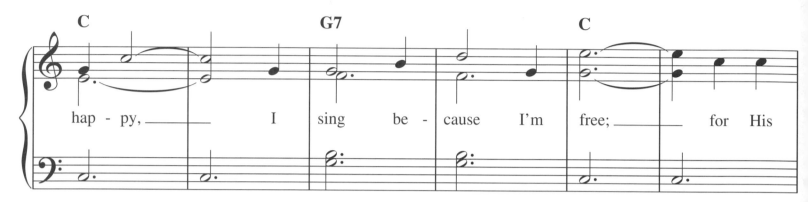

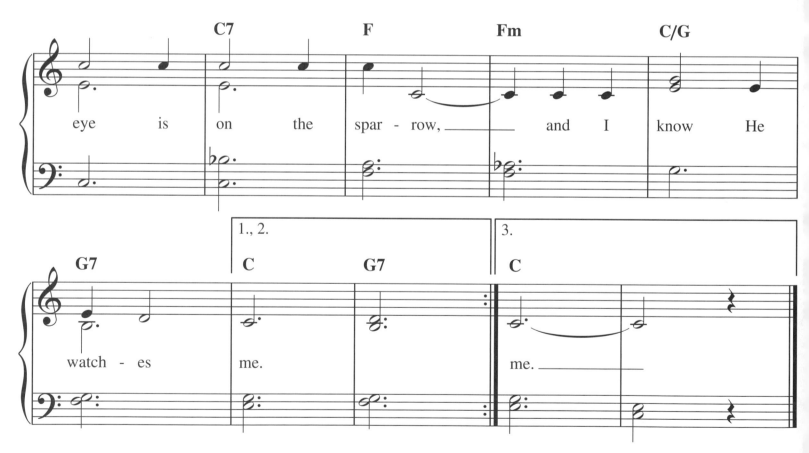

Additional Lyrics

3. Whenever I am tempted,
   Whenever clouds arise,
   When song gives place to sighing,
   When hope within me dies,
   I draw the closer to Him,
   From care He sets me free:
   Refrain

I WILL FOLLOW HIM
(I Will Follow You)

English Words by NORMAN GIMBEL and ARTHUR ALTMAN
French Words by JACQUES PLANTE
Music by J.W. STOLE and DEL ROMA

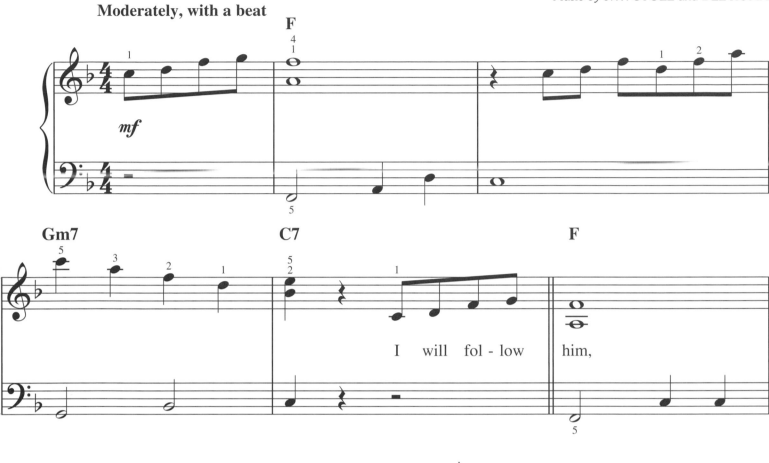

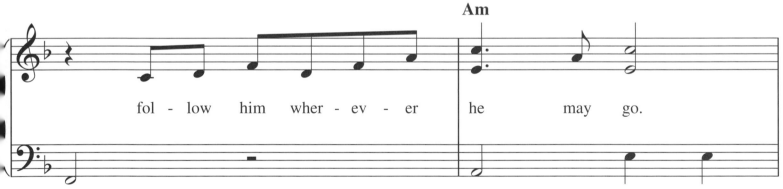

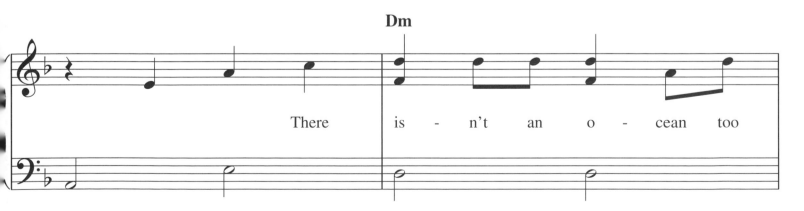

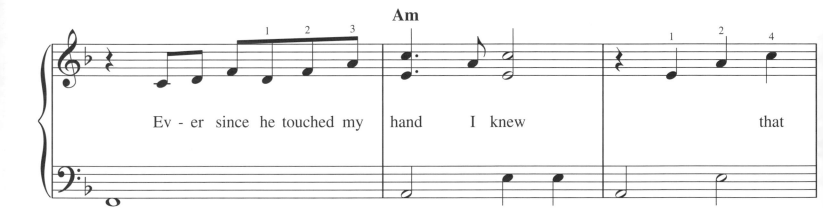

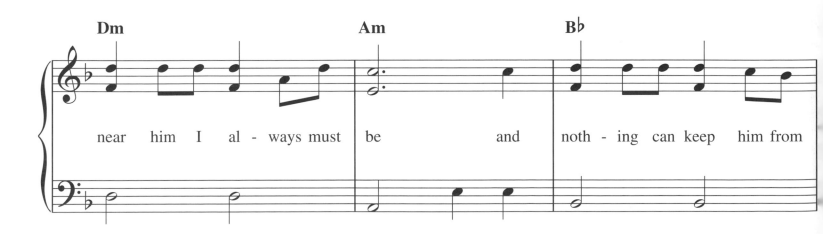

me, he is my des - tin - y. I

love him, I love him, I love him and where he goes I'll

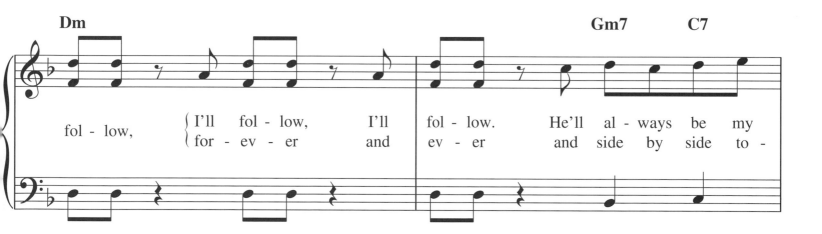

fol - low, { I'll fol - low, I'll fol - low. He'll al - ways be my
for - ev - er and ev - er and side by side to -

true love, my true love, my true love, from now un - til for -
geth - er I'll be with my true love, and share a thou - sand

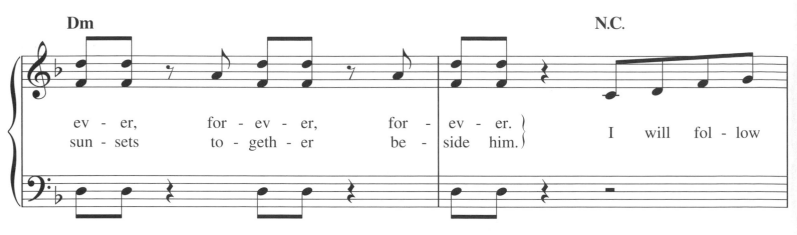

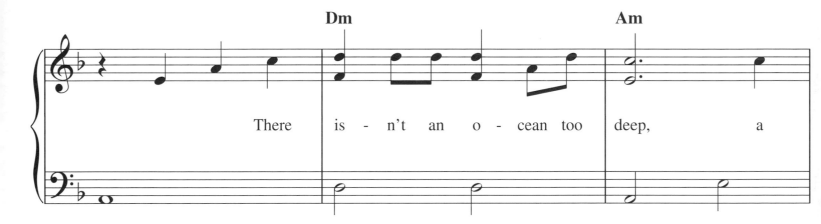

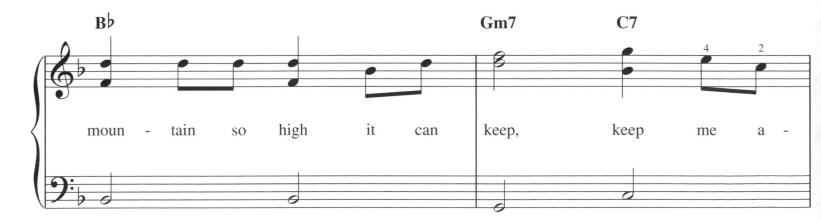

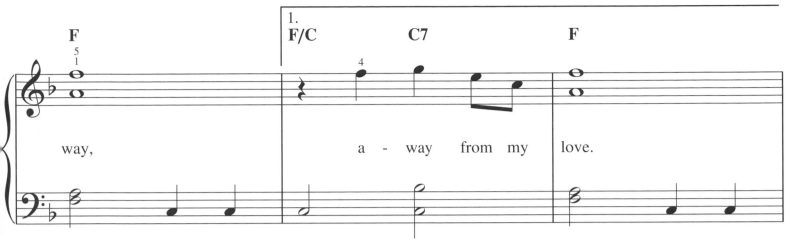

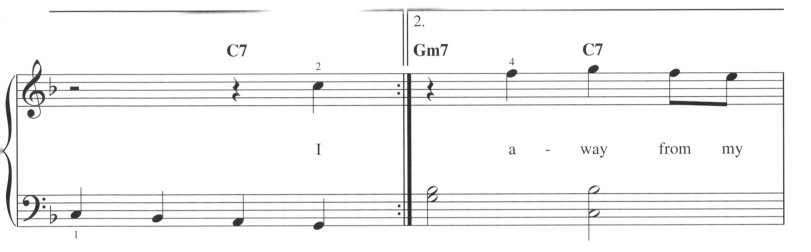

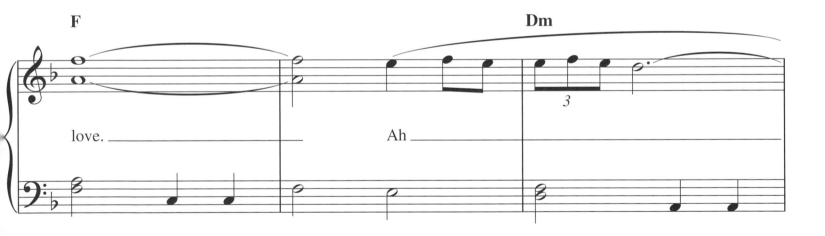

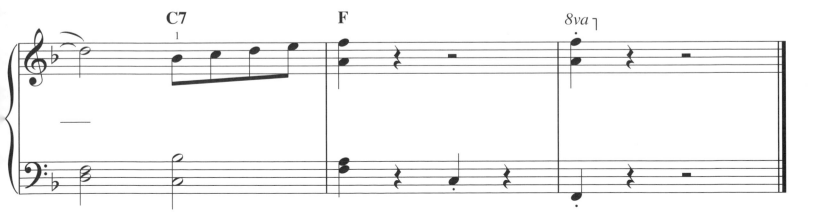

JOYFUL, JOYFUL

Arranged by MERVYN WARREN
Based on LUDWIG VAN BEETHOVEN'S "SYMPHONY NO. 9"
Additional rap lyrics by RYAN TOBY

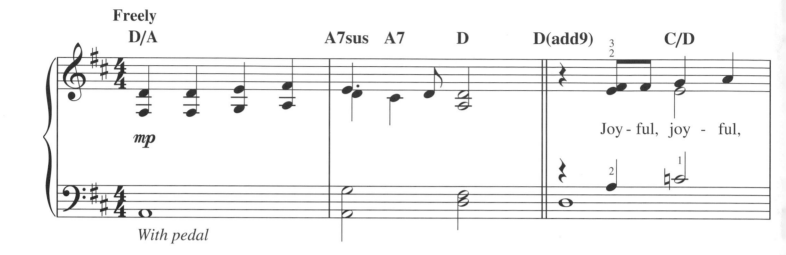

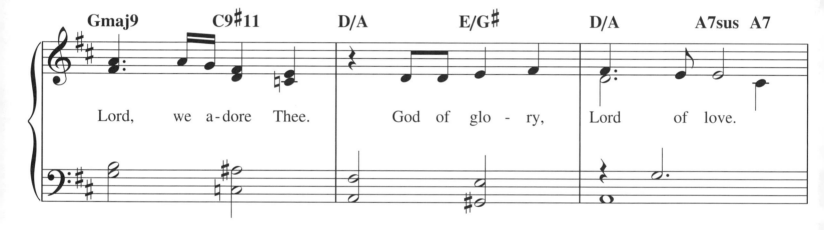

Joy - ful, joy - ful, Lord, we a-dore Thee. God of glo - ry, Lord of love.

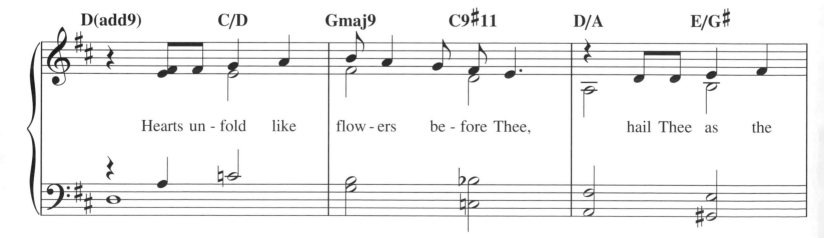

Hearts un - fold like flow - ers be - fore Thee, hail Thee as the

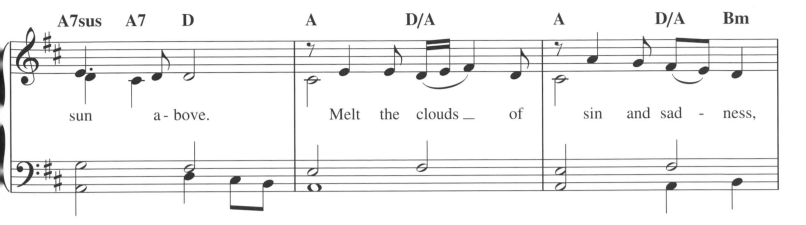

sun a-bove. Melt the clouds __ of sin and sad - ness,

drive the dark of doubt a - way. Giv - er of im -

rit.

mor - tal glad - ness, fill us with the light. _____

rit.

Fill us with the light. Oh, fill __ us with the light of

molto rit.

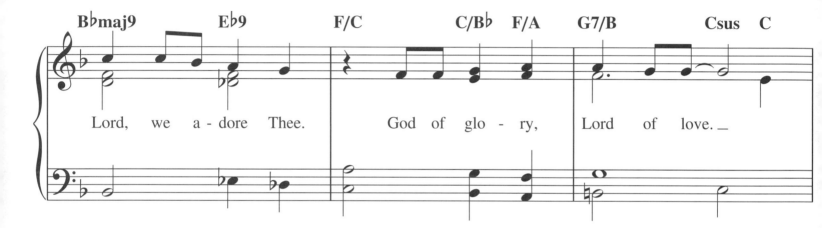

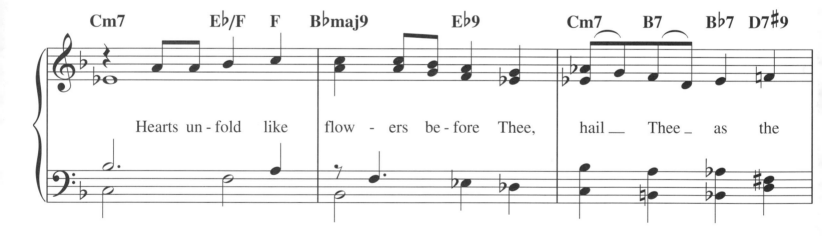

Drive the __ dark of doubt a - way, drive it a - way. Giv - er of im - mor -

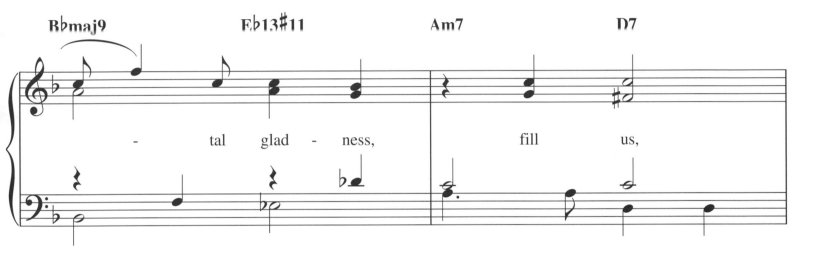

- tal glad - ness, fill us,

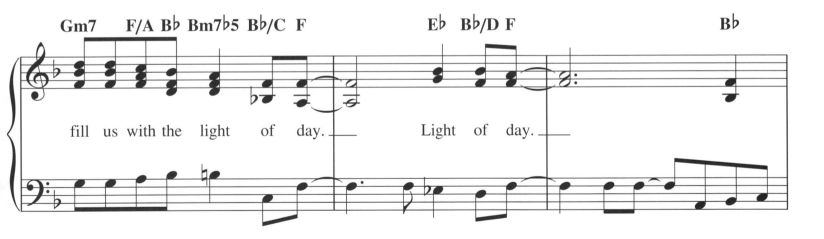

fill us with the light of day. __ Light of day. __

(See Rap lyrics)

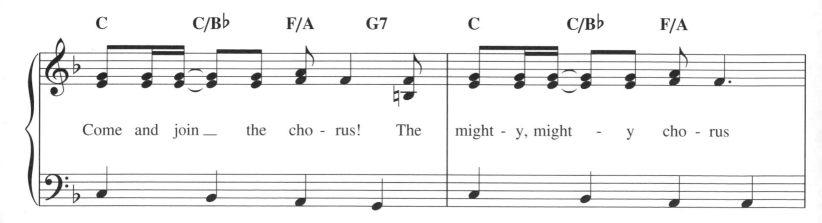

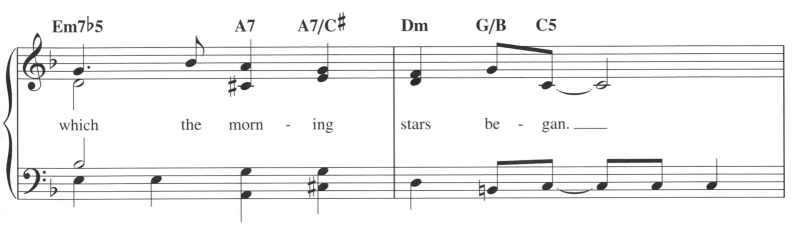

Em7♭5 ... **A7** ... **A7/C♯** ... **Dm** ... **G/B** ... **C5**

which the morn - ing stars be - gan. ___

Cm7 ... **E♭/F** ... **F** ... **B♭maj9** ... **E♭13♯11** ... **Fm6** ... **Fm**

The Fa-ther of Love is reign - ing o - ver us. What have you

Fm6

done for Him late - ly? Oo ___ yeah!

Fm ... **Dm7** ... **G7**

What have you done for Him late - ly? He watch-es o - ver

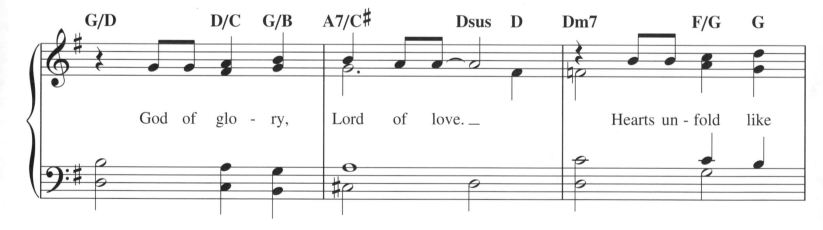

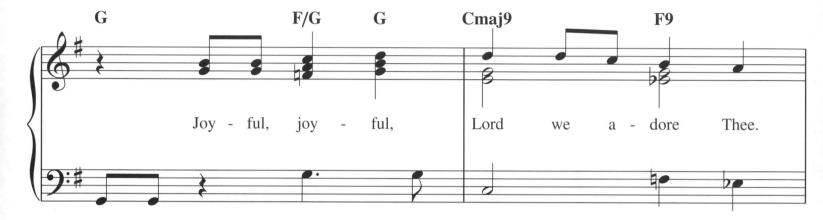

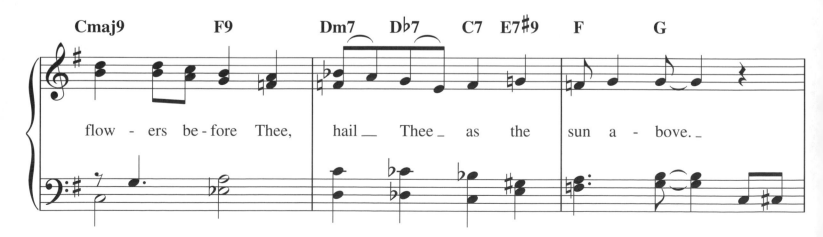

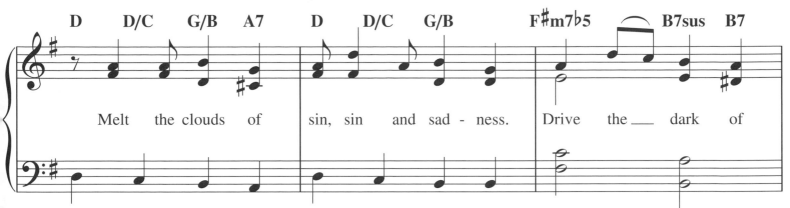

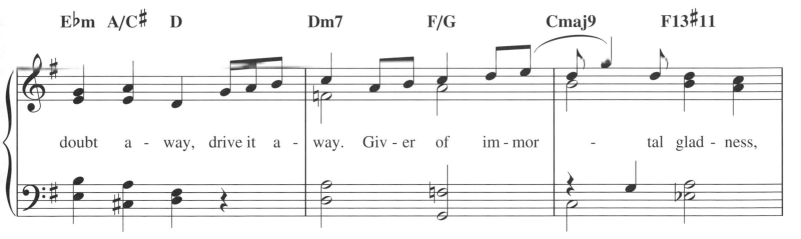

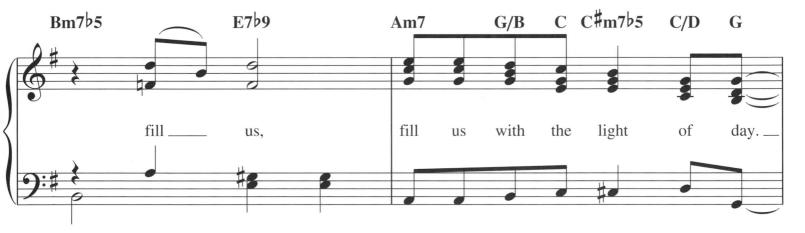

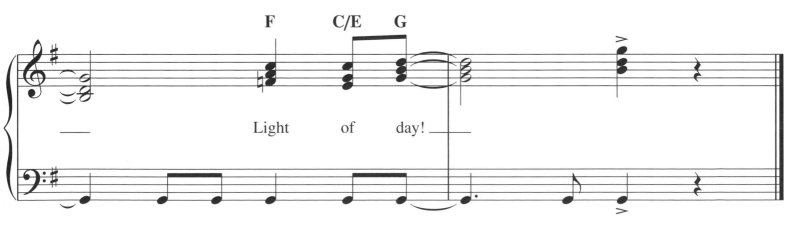

Rap Lyrics

Check the rhyme: Joyful! Joyful! Lord, we adore Thee, and in my life I put none before Thee.
'Cause since I was a youngster, I came to know that You was the only way to go. So, I have to grow
with, come to an understanding. Then I'm down with the King, so I'm demanding that you tell me
who you are. See, 'cause all I know is that I'm down with G-O-D.

JUST A TOUCH OF LOVE
(Everyday)

Words and Music by
ROBERT CLIVILLES

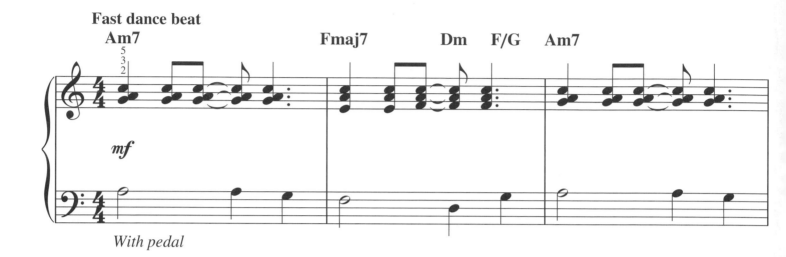

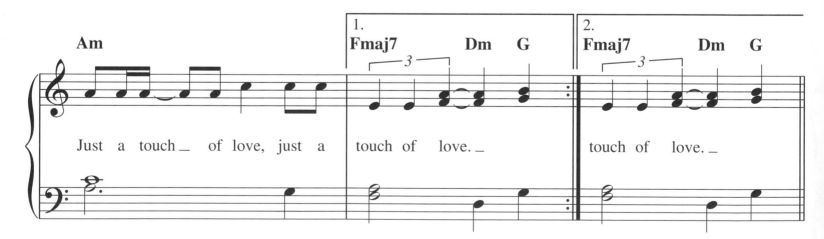

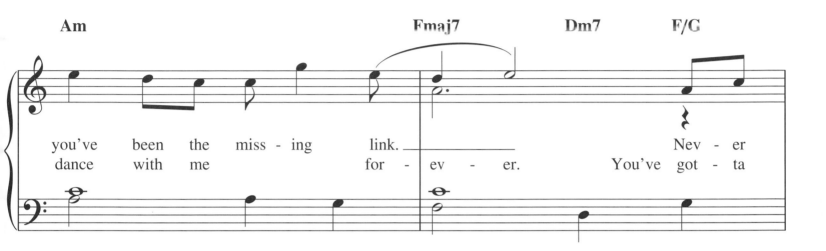

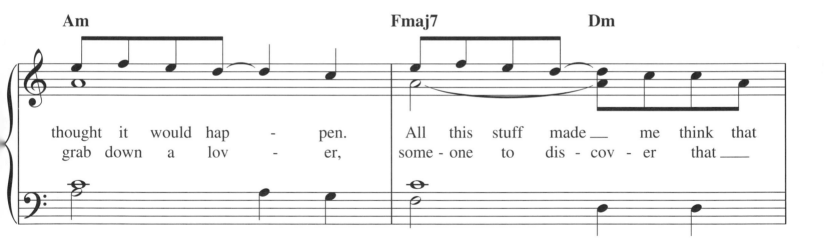

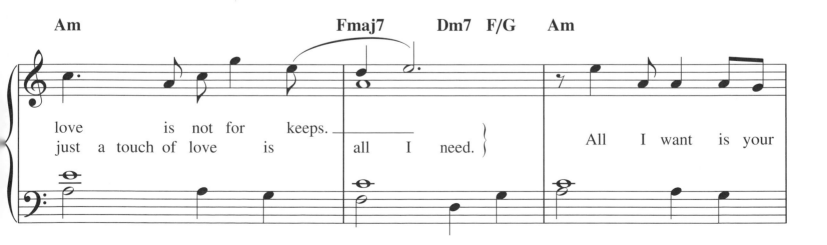

touch of love. __ Just a touch __ of love, just a touch of love. __

touch of love. __ Just a touch __ of love, just a touch of love. __

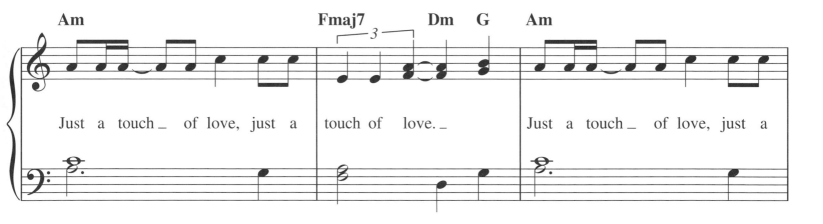

Just a touch __ of love, just a touch of love. __ Just a touch __ of love, just a

touch of love. __ Just a touch __ of love, just a touch of love. _____

MY GUY (MY GOD)

Words and Music by
WILLIAM "SMOKEY" ROBINSON

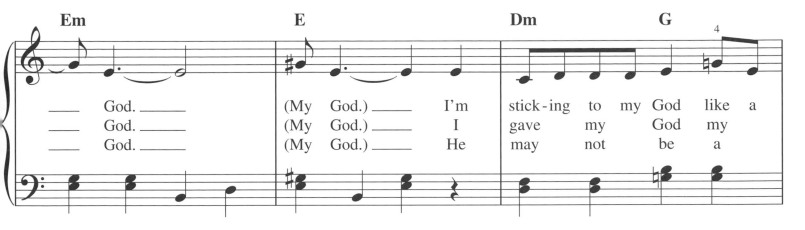

God. (My God.) I'm stick-ing to my God like a
God. (My God.) I gave my God my
God. (My God.) He may not be a

stamp to a let - ter. Like birds of a feath - er, we
word of hon - or to be faith - ful,
mov - ie star, but when it comes to be - in' hap - py,

stick to - geth - er. I'm tell - in' you from the start, I can't
and I'm gon - na. You best be be - liev - ing I won't

1.

be torn a - part from my God.
be de - ceiv - ing my God.

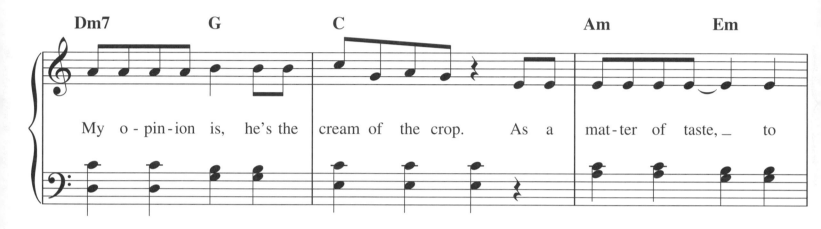

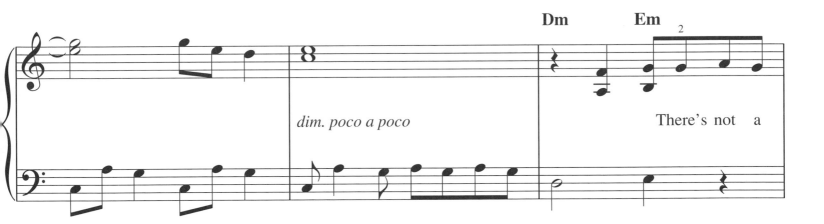

NEVER SHOULD'VE LET YOU GO

Words and Music by
ERIC FOSTER WHITE

Took for grant-ed the love you gave___ and on - ly thought of the
I don't blame you for leav - ing me,___ but now you've got to be -

love we made. Just when I found some-one who could love me___ like the
lieve in me. If you come back,___ girl, I prom - ise___ that you'll

way that I need,___ I act - ed the
see a change in my ways.___ I'll get down on my

fool and pushed her a - way from me.___ And I'll be
knees. I'll do an - y - thing you say.

B♭ **B♭7** **E♭** **E♭/F**

think - ing 'bout you ev - er - y night and ev - 'ry day, —

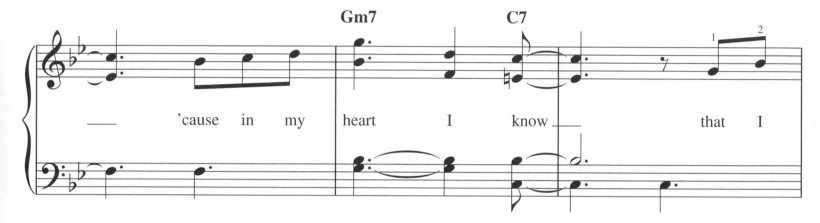

Gm7 **C7**

— 'cause in my heart I know___ that I

E♭ **B♭/D** **Cm7** **E♭/F** **B♭**

nev - er should - 've let you go. __ And my love for you is

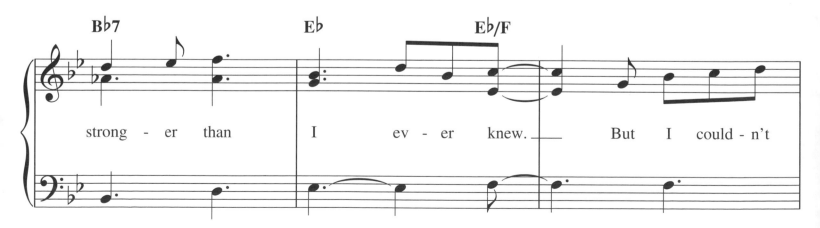

B♭7 **E♭** **E♭/F**

strong - er than I ev - er knew. __ But I could - n't

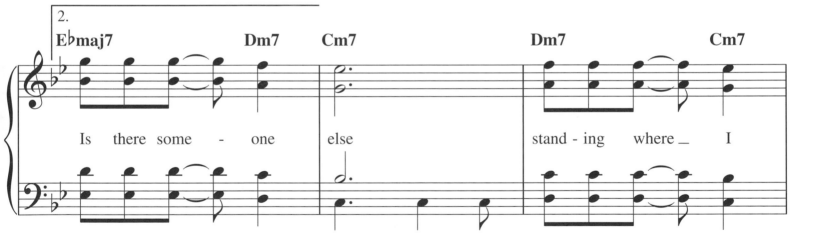

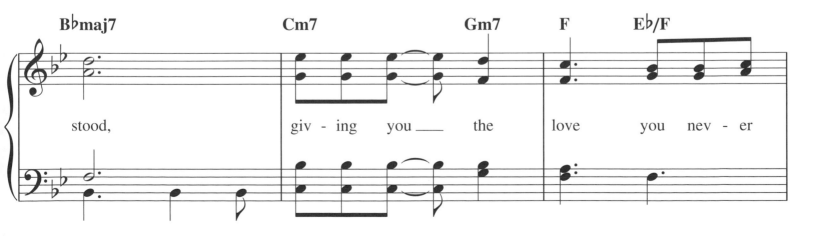

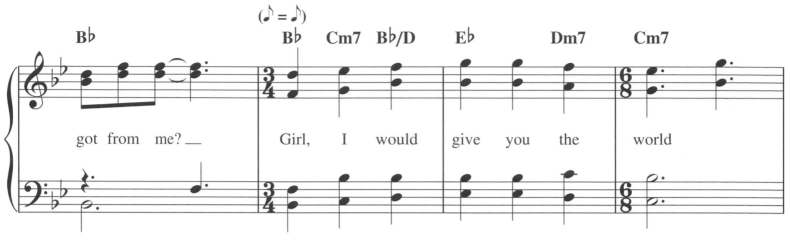

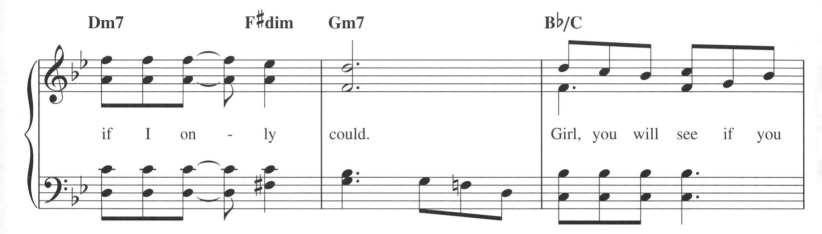

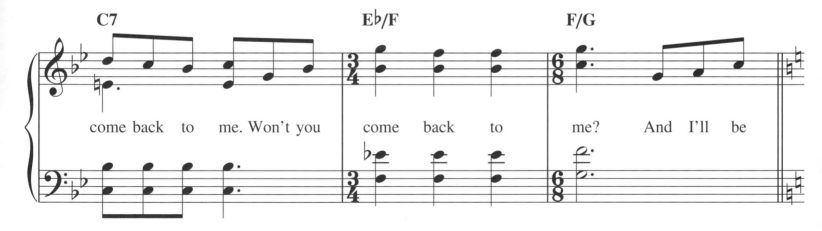

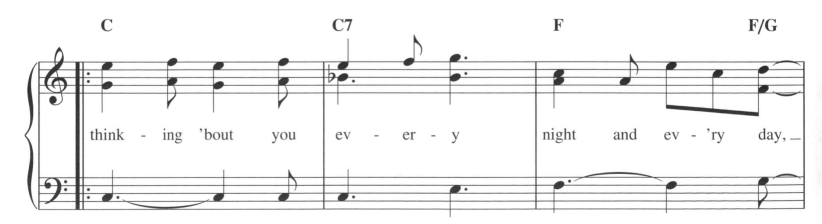

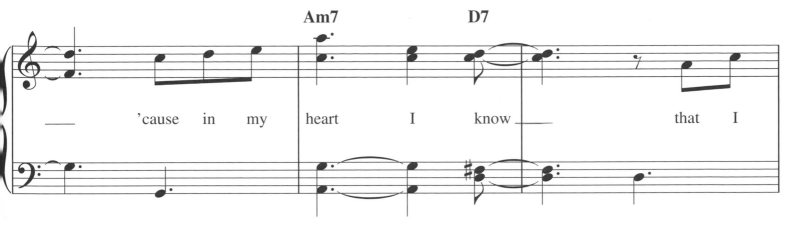

'cause in my heart I know _____ that I

nev - er should - 've let you go. _____ And my love for you is

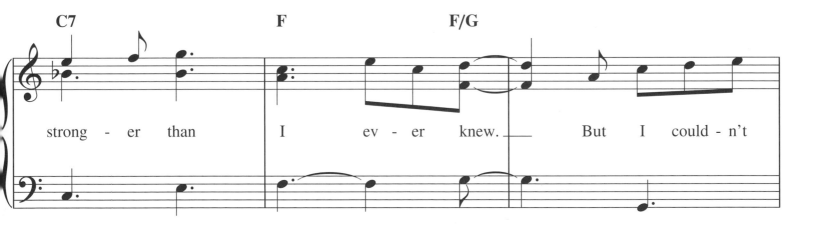

strong - er than I ev - er knew. _____ But I could - n't

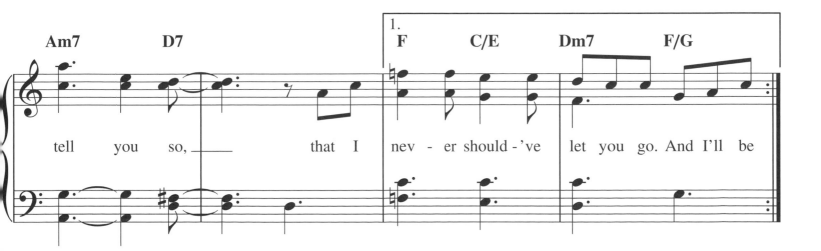

tell you so, _____ that I nev - er should - 've let you go. And I'll be

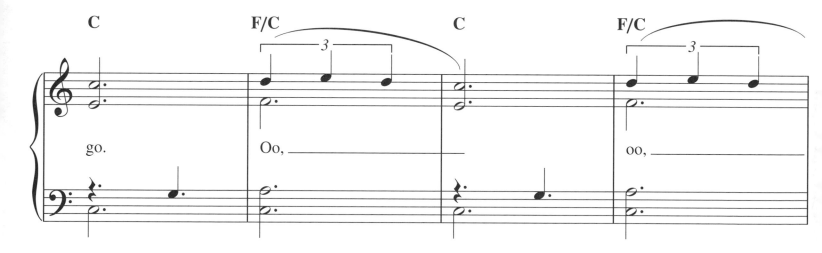

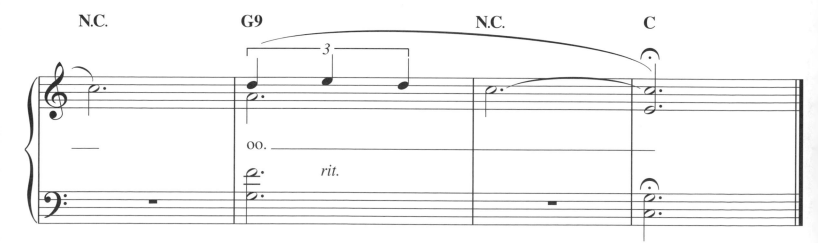

OH HAPPY DAY

Words and Music by
EDWIN R. HAWKINS

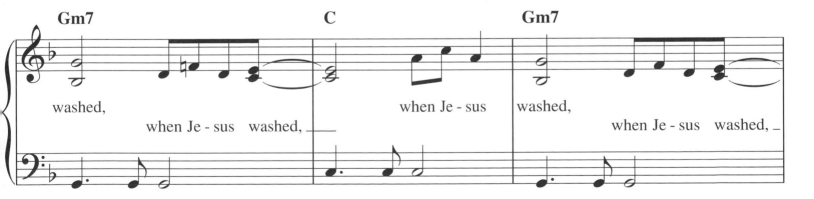

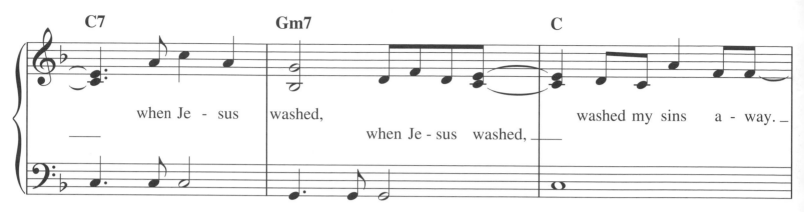

La la la la la la la.   La la la la la.   La la la la la.

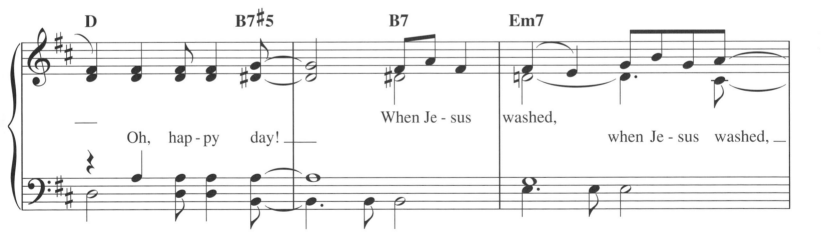

G/A   D   G/D

Oh, __ hap-py day! __   Oh, hap-py day! __   Oh, hap-py day! __

D   B7#5   B7   Em7

Oh, hap-py day! __   When Je - sus washed,   when Je - sus washed, __

A7   Em7   A7

when Je - sus washed,   when Je - sus washed, __   when __ Je - sus

washed,
when Je-sus washed,
he washed my sins _ a - way.
La la la la la la la.

La la la la la la la.
La la la la la.
La la la la la.

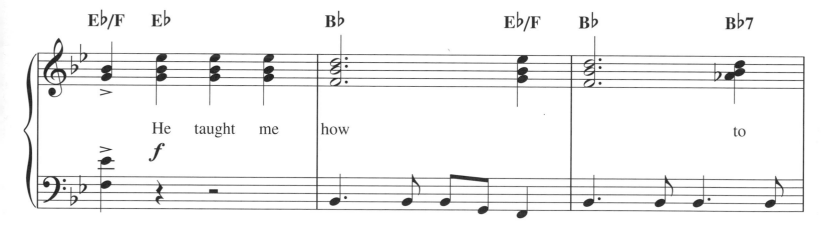

He taught me how
to

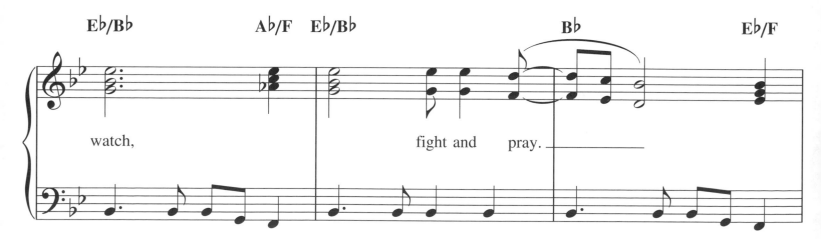

watch,
fight and pray. _

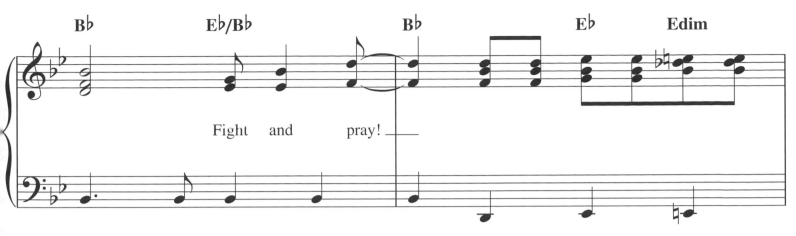

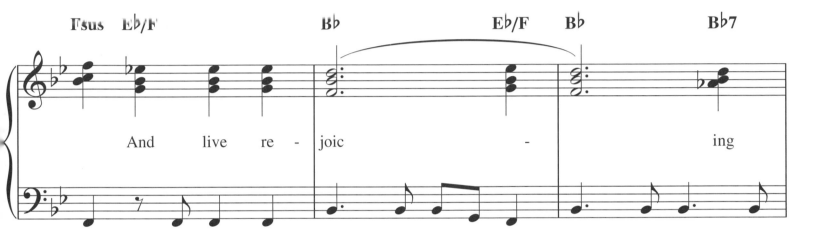

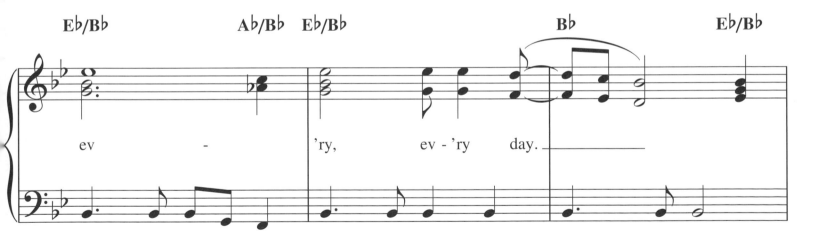

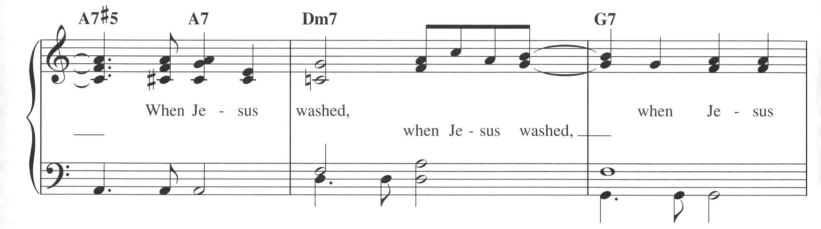

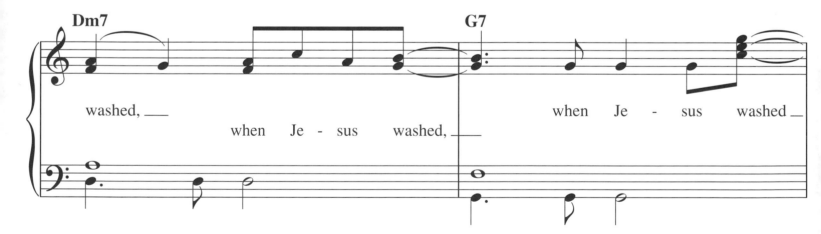

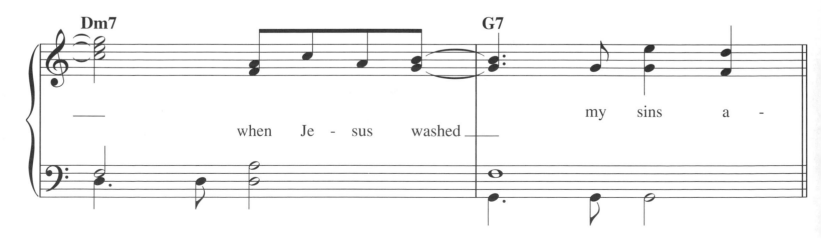

way.
Oh, hap - py day! I'm talk - ing 'bout that

hap - py day!
Oh, hap - py day! Oh, hap - py day!

Oh, hap - py day!

Oh, hap - py day! Oh, hap - py day!

RESCUE ME

Words and Music by RAYNARD MINER
and CARL SMITH

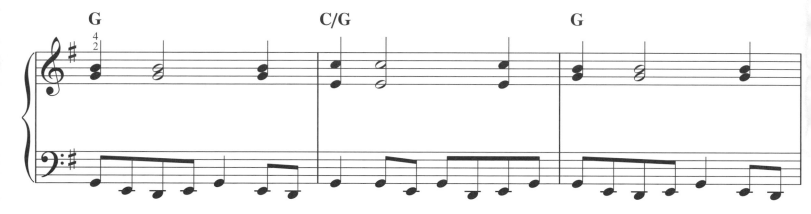

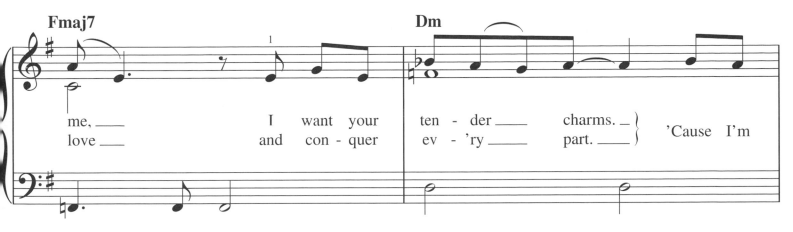

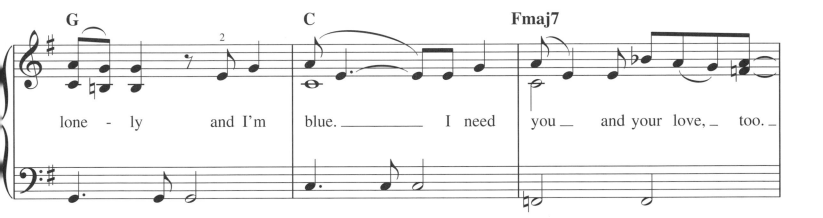

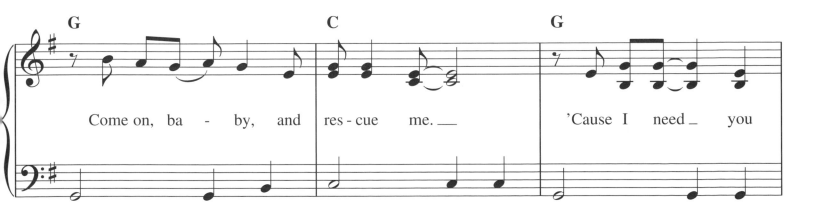

by my side. _____ Can't you see ____ that I'm

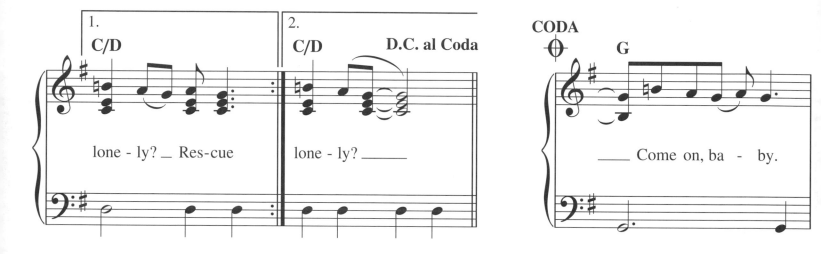

1.
lone - ly? _ Res-cue

2.
lone - ly? _____

CODA
____ Come on, ba - by.

Take me, ba - by.   Hold me, ba - by.   Love me, ba - by.

Can't you see ___ that I   need _ you, ba - by?   Can't you see ___ that I'm

lone - ly? ___ Res - cue me, come on and take my hand. ___

Come on, ba - by, and be my man, ___ 'cause I love ___ you,

'cause I want ___ you. ___ Can't you see ___ that I'm

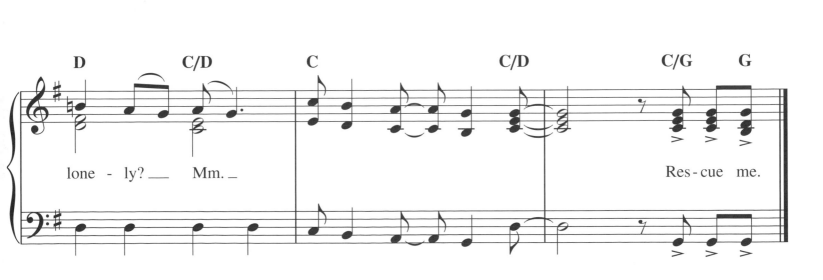

lone - ly? ___ Mm. ___ Res - cue me.

SHOUT

Words and Music by O'KELLY ISLEY,
RONALD ISLEY and RUDOLPH ISLEY

will.) Say it right now, ba - by. (Say you will.) Come on, ___ come

on. (Say you will.) Say that you... ___ (Say you

will.) (Say!) Say that you love me. (Say!) Say that you need me.

(Say!) Say that you want me. Say you wan - na please me.

(Say!) Come on, ___ now. ___   (Say!) Come on, ___ now. ___   (Say!) Come on, ___ now. ___

(Say!)   I still re - mem-ber   when I   used to be ___ nine years

old,   hey ___ yeah.   And I was a   fool for you   from the

bot - tom   of my   soul, ___ yeah ___ yeah. ___   Now that I

found you, I will nev - er let you go, _____ no, _____

no. _ And if you ev - er leave me, you know it's gon - na hurt me

Moderate Shuffle

so. I want you to know,

I said, I want you to know _ right now. You been good _ to me,

sis - ters, _____ much bet - ter than I been to my - self, so good, _ so good. _

_ And if _ you ev - er leave me, _ I don't want no - bod - y

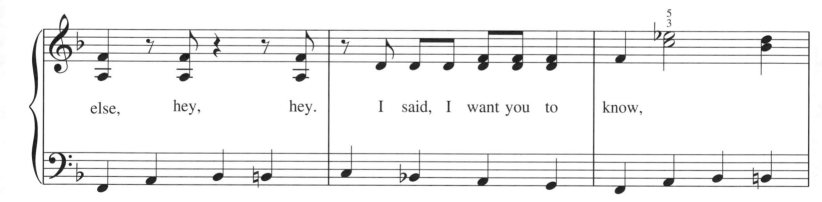

else, hey, hey. I said, I want you to know,

Lively Rock (Tempo I)

yeah. I said, I want you to know right now. _ You know you make me wan-na

(Shout!) pick my heels _ up and (Shout!) throw my hands _ up and (Shout!) throw my head _ back and

(Shout!) come on, ___ now. Hey, _____

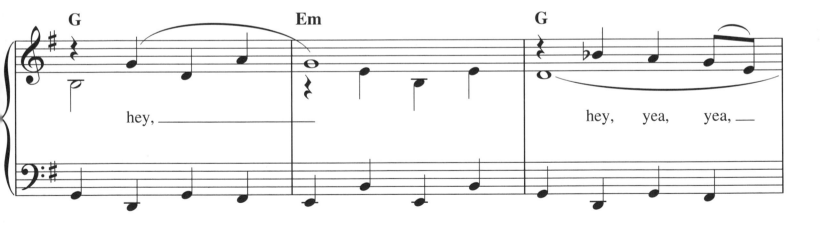

hey, _____ hey, yea, yea, ___

yea. (Hey, yea, yea, __ yea.) Hey, yea, yea, __ yea. (Hey, yea, yea.) _

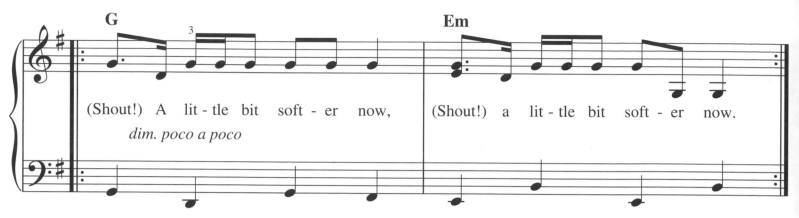

G   3   **Em**

(Shout!) A lit - tle bit soft - er now,   (Shout!) a lit - tle bit soft - er now.

dim. poco a poco

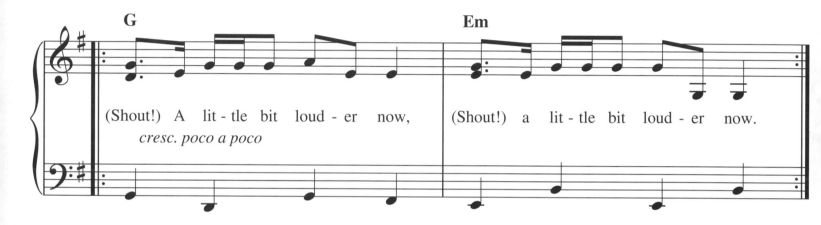

G   **Em**

(Shout!) A lit - tle bit loud - er now,   (Shout!) a lit - tle bit loud - er now.

cresc. poco a poco

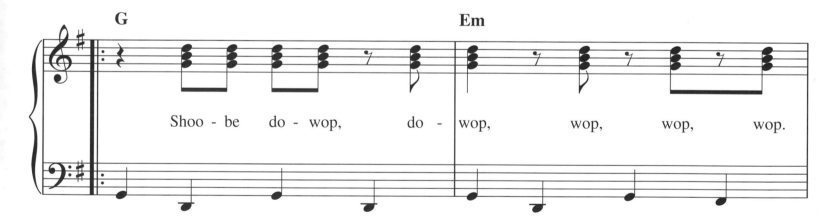

G   **Em**

Shoo - be do - wop,   do - wop,   wop,   wop,   wop.

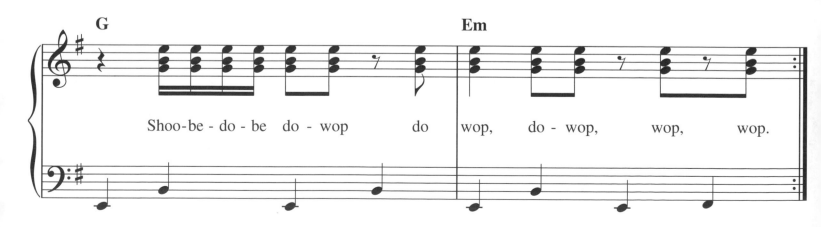

G   **Em**

Shoo - be - do - be do - wop   do wop,   do - wop,   wop,   wop.

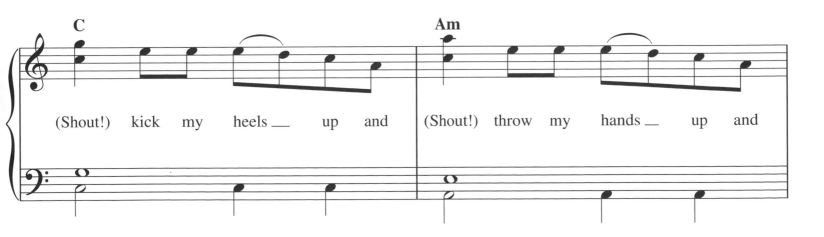

(Shout!) throw my head _ back and (Shout!) come on, ___ now. ___ Don't for-get to say you

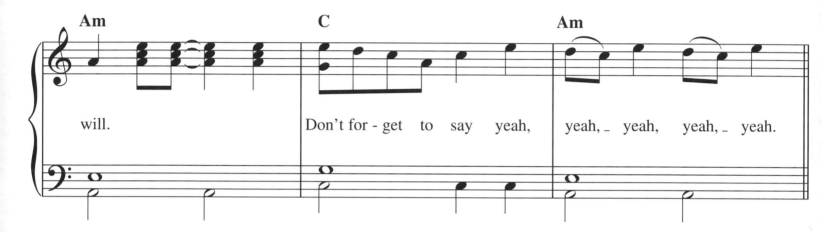

will. Don't for-get to say yeah, yeah, _ yeah, yeah, _ yeah.

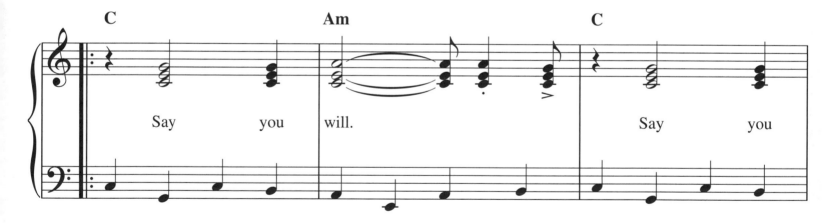

Say you will. Say you

will. _____ You know you make me wan-na shout.